WOULD YOU RATHER COUPLES

FOR NAUGHTY, KINKY COUPLES

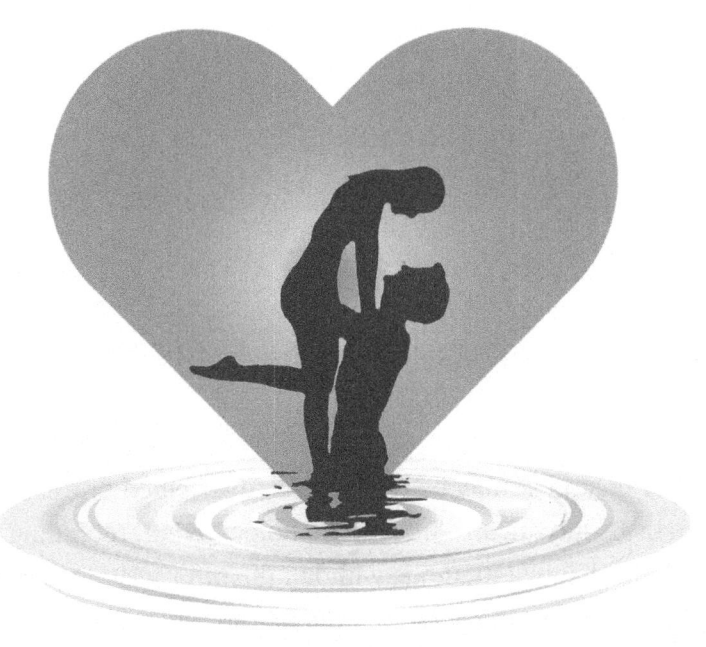

Copyright © 2023 Relight Publishing All rights reserved.

No part of this book may be reproduced, distributed or transmitted in any form or by any means, including photocopying, recording, or other electric or mechanical methods without, the prior written permission of the publisher, except in the case of quotations embodied in reviews and certain other non-commercial uses permitted by copyright law.

Published by Relight Publishing

ISBN: 9798376647066

Message from the Author

Would You Rather first appeared in psychological studies in the 1960s. Evidence suggests that in the 1970s the game was used to study the aggressive behavior in some children. By the year 2000 Would You Rather has become a well known conversational party game and it's various formats are known throughout the world.

In this edition the game focuses on couples their sexual appetites. *Would You Rather Couples* offers the opportunity to know your partners deep desires and sexual fantasies along with the chance to spark healthy debates among lovers. The book is very engaging and the funny scenarios will make you both laugh out loud.

There are 102 themes inside the book where each of the couples has a turn a selecting which scenario they would prefer. The game is incredibly fun to play and very addictive. We have included some very obscure topics for your entertainment and hope you will find them amusing.

Each player takes a turn in asking their partner which scenario they would prefer. You can play the game anyhow you like, starting from front to back or vise versa. There is no correct format, just have fun.

Please enjoy the book and look out for future publications

"EVERYTHING IN THE WORLD IS ABOUT SEX EXCEPT SEX. SEX IS ABOUT POWER."

~Oscar Wilde~

1.

WOULD YOU RATHER

HOOKUP ON THE BEACH

OR

HOOKUP ON THE DANCE FLOOR?

2.

WOULD YOU RATHER

BE A 10 IN TERMS OF LOOKS

OR

A 10 IN BED?

3.

WOULD YOU RATHER

HAVE A PARTNER WHO'S A 10 IN LOOKS

OR

WHO'S A 10 IN BED?

4.

WOULD YOU RATHER

MARRY SOMEONE WITH NO SEXUAL EXPERIENCE

OR

A LOT OF SEXUAL EXPERIENCE?

5.

WOULD YOU RATHER

ALWAYS BE ON TOP

OR

ALWAYS BE AT THE BOTTOM?

6.

WOULD YOU RATHER

HAVE SEX EARLY IN THE MORNING

OR

LATE AT NIGHT?

7.

WOULD YOU RATHER

RECEIVE A SEXY PHOTO

OR

A SEXY PHONE CALL?

8.

WOULD YOU RATHER

HAVE REALLY KINKY SEX

OR

REALLY ROMANTIC SEX?

9.

WOULD YOU RATHER

GIVE UP KISSING

OR

SEX FOR THE REST OF YOUR LIFE?

10.

WOULD YOU RATHER

HAVE ONLY ORAL

OR

ONLY INTERCOURSE FOR THE REST OF YOUR LIFE?

11.

WOULD YOU RATHER

HAVE THE BEST SEX OF YOUR LIFE TOMORROW

OR

IN 10 YEARS?

12.

WOULD YOU RATHER

HAVE AVERAGE SEX EVERY DAY

OR

AMAZING SEX ONCE A MONTH?

13.

WOULD YOU RATHER

HAVE SUPER-HOT SEX BUT NOT ORGASM

OR

HAVE OKAY SEX AND GET TO CUM?

14.

WOULD YOU RATHER

HAVE SEX IN THE CAR

OR

SEX IN A BATHROOM?

15.

WOULD YOU RATHER

HAVE CAMPING SEX

OR

SHOWER SEX?

16.

WOULD YOU RATHER

HAVE AIRPLANE SEX

OR

ELEVATOR SEX?

17.

WOULD YOU RATHER

DOMINATE

OR

BE DOMINATED?

18.

WOULD YOU RATHER

BE TREATED LIKE A GOOD PERSON

OR

A NAUGHTY PERSON IN BED?

19.

WOULD YOU RATHER

HAVE SEX WITH A TEACHER

OR

A BOSS?

20.

WOULD YOU RATHER

WATCH PEOPLE HAVING SEX

OR

BE WATCHED WHILE YOU'RE HAVING SEX?

21.

WOULD YOU RATHER

SWAP PARTNERS WITH ANOTHER COUPLE

OR

HAVE A THREESOME?

22.

WOULD YOU RATHER

HAVE SEX WITH YOUR CELEBRITY CRUSH

OR

YOUR HIGH SCHOOL CRUSH?

23.

WOULD YOU RATHER

TRY ROPE PLAY

OR

ROLE PLAY?

24.

WOULD YOU RATHER

HAVE FOOD INCORPORATED INTO SEX

OR

A BLINDFOLD INCORPORATED INTO SEX?

25.

WOULD YOU RATHER

HAVE IT FAST AND HARD

OR

SLOW AND SENSUAL?

26.

WOULD YOU RATHER

BE BLINDFOLDED DURING SEX

OR

OR HAVE YOUR PARTNER WEAR THE BLINDFOLD?

27.

WOULD YOU RATHER

TRY A NEW SEX POSITION

OR

TRY A NEW KINK?

28.

WOULD YOU RATHER

HAVE SEX THAT LASTED TWO MINUTES

OR

TWO HOURS?

29.

WOULD YOU RATHER

USE ICE CUBES

OR

CANDLE WAX IN BED?

30.

WOULD YOU RATHER

NEVER MASTURBATE AGAIN

OR

NEVER HAVE SEX AGAIN?

31.

WOULD YOU RATHER

WATCH YOUR PARTNER MASTURBATE

OR

HAVE YOUR PARTNER WATCH YOU MASTURBATE?

32.

WOULD YOU RATHER

HAVE SEX IN THE PARK

OR

SEX IN THE WOODS?

33.

WOULD YOU RATHER

NEVER KISS AGAIN

OR

NEVER HAVE ORAL SEX AGAIN?

34.

WOULD YOU RATHER

BE SPANKED

OR

DO THE SPANKING?

35.

WOULD YOU RATHER

TALK DiRTY

OR

BE TALKED DiRTY TO?

36.

WOULD YOU RATHER

HAVE PHONE SEX

OR

ViDEO CALL SEX?

37.

WOULD YOU RATHER

YOUR PARTNER TAKE YOUR CLOTHES OFF SLOWLY

OR

TEAR THEM OFF IN A FIT OF PASSION?

38.

WOULD YOU RATHER

HAVE SEX ON A SOFA

OR

ON AN ARM CHAIR?

39.

WOULD YOU RATHER

WEAR A KINKY COSTUME TO BED

OR

USE SEX TOYS?

40.

WOULD YOU RATHER

HAVE SEX IN THE BACK OF A CAB

OR

IN A PUBLIC PARK?

41.

WOULD YOU RATHER

NEVER HAVE ORAL SEX AGAIN

OR

NEVER HAVE PENETRATIVE SEX AGAIN?

42.

WOULD YOU RATHER

BUY A SEX TOY

OR

BUY AN ADULT FILM?

43.

WOULD YOU RATHER

RECEIVE NUDES

OR

SEND NUDES

44.

WOULD YOU RATHER

HAVE YOUR HANDS TIED DURING SEX

OR

WEAR A BLINDFOLD DURING SEX?

45.

WOULD YOU RATHER

ALWAYS DO IT WITH THE LIGHTS ON

OR

ALWAYS DO IT WITH THE LIGHTS OFF?

46.

WOULD YOU RATHER

BE VOCAL FOR THE DURATION OF SEX

OR

STAY SILENT THE ENTIRE TIME?

47.

WOULD YOU RATHER

HAVE SEX WHEN IT'S REALLY COLD

OR

WHEN IT'S REALLY HOT?

48.

WOULD YOU RATHER

HAVE QUICKIE SEX A FEW TIMES A WEEK

OR

ONE LONG PASSIONATE SESSION ONCE A MONTH?

49.

WOULD YOU RATHER

TELL YOUR PARTNER YOU DEEPEST SEX FANTASY

OR

HEAR ABOUT YOUR PARTNER'S DEEPEST SEX FANTASY?

50.

WOULD YOU RATHER

HAVE YOUR HAIR PULLED

OR

YOUR NIPPLES PINCHED?

51.

WOULD YOU RATHER

ALWAYS HAVE SEX UNDER THE COVERS

OR

NEVER HAVE SEX UNDER THE COVERS?

52.

WOULD YOU RATHER

GIVE A LAP DANCE

OR

RECEIVE A LAP DANCE?

53.

WOULD YOU RATHER

HAVE A PARTNER WHO IS PASSIVE

OR

AGGRESSIVE?

54.

WOULD YOU RATHER

END A FIRST DATE WITH A KISS

OR

WITH A HUG?

55.

WOULD YOU RATHER

YOUR NEIGHBORS SEE YOU NAKED

OR

YOU SEE THEM NAKED?

56.

WOULD YOU RATHER

YOUR PARTNER BE KINKY

OR

ROMANTIC?

57.

WOULD YOU RATHER

SLEEP WITH YOUR PARTNER'S SIBLINGS

OR

YOUR BEST FRIEND'S SIBLING?

58.

WOULD YOU RATHER

GET A JOB PROMOTION

OR

SLEEP WITH YOUR HOT COLLEAGUE?

59.

WOULD YOU RATHER

BE IN A LOVELESS MARRIAGE

OR

A SEXLESS MARRIAGE?

60.

WOULD YOU RATHER

BE IN A COMMITTED RELATIONSHIP

OR

BE FRIENDS WITH BENEFITS?

61.

WOULD YOU RATHER

HAVE A ONE-NIGHT STAND WITH A STRANGER

OR

YOUR PLATONIC BEST FRIEND?

62.

WOULD YOU RATHER

HAVE SEX IN PUBLIC

OR

IN A SECRET HIDING PLACE?

63.

WOULD YOU RATHER

HAVE A LACKLUSTER PROPOSAL iN BED

OR

NO PROPOSAL AT ALL?

64.

WOULD YOU RATHER

ACCiDENTALLY SEND NUDES TO A STRANGER

OR

YOUR PARENTS?

65.

WOULD YOU RATHER

MAKE OUT WITH SOMEONE AT A NIGHTCLUB

OR

MAKE OUT WITH SOMEONE AT A WORK?

66.

WOULD YOU RATHER

BE SURPRISED IN BED

OR

ALWAYS KNOW WHAT'S COMING?

67.

WOULD YOU RATHER

BE NAKED

OR

WEAR FULL-COVERAGE UNDERWEAR?

68.

WOULD YOU RATHER

WEAR COMFY CLOTHES

OR

SEXY CLOTHES TO BED?

69.

WOULD YOU RATHER

BE FINANCIALLY SATISFIED

OR

SEXUALLY SATISFIED?

70.

WOULD YOU RATHER

ACCIDENTALLY SCREAM THE WRONG NAME IN BED

OR

HAVE YOUR PARTNER ACCIDENTALLY SCREAM THE WRONG NAME IN BED?

11.

WOULD YOU RATHER

WALK IN ON YOUR PARENTS

OR

HAVE YOUR PARENTS WALK IN ON YOU?

12.

WOULD YOU RATHER

BE FLIRTY

OR

FUNNY?

13.

WOULD YOU RATHER

HAVE YOUR HAIR PULLED

OR

YOUR BUTT SMACKED?

14.

WOULD YOU RATHER

GET A GOOD MORNING TEXT

OR

GOOD NIGHT TEXT?

75.

WOULD YOU RATHER

GRANT ROMANTIC WISHES

OR

HAVE YOUR OWN ROMANTIC WISHES GRANTED?

76.

WOULD YOU RATHER

SHOWER TOGETHER

OR

APART?

77.

WOULD YOU RATHER

STAY IN

OR

GO OUT?

78.

WOULD YOU RATHER

READ 50 SHADES OF GREY

OR

WATCH 50 SHADES OF GREY?

79.

WOULD YOU RATHER

BE CALLED ICY

OR

OVERLY EMOTIONAL?

80.

WOULD YOU RATHER

GO ON A ROMANTIC GETAWAY TOGETHER

OR

GO ON A SHORT VACATION BY YOURSELF?

81.

WOULD YOU RATHER

BRING FOOD INTO THE BEDROOM

OR

PROPS?

82.

WOULD YOU RATHER

COVER YOUR PARTNER IN EDIBLE BODY PAINT

OR

HAVE THEM WEAR EDIBLE UNDERGARMENTS?

83.

WOULD YOU RATHER

BE SNOWED IN WITH YOUR CRUSH

OR

LAY ON THE BEACH WITH YOUR CRUSH?

84.

WOULD YOU RATHER

GO WATCH A MOVIE

OR

GO WATCH THE SUNSET?

85.

WOULD YOU RATHER

KISS IN PUBLIC

OR

KISS IN PRIVATE?

86.

WOULD YOU RATHER

LET YOUR PARTNER DATE YOUR BEST FRIEND

OR

YOUR ARCH ENEMY?

87.

WOULD YOU RATHER

BE WITH A JEALOUS HARDWORKING PARTNER

OR

A LAZY BUT TRUSTING PARTNER?

88.

WOULD YOU RATHER

SNEEZE EVERY TIME YOU ORGASM

OR

ORGASM EVERY TIME YOU SNEEZE?

89.

WOULD YOU RATHER

SPIT

OR

SWALLOW?

90.

WOULD YOU RATHER

BE CHEATED ON BY A PARTNER

OR

CHEAT ON A PARTNER?

91.

WOULD YOU RATHER

BE KISSED ON THE LIPS OVER AND OVER

OR

BE KISSED ALL OVER?

92.

WOULD YOU RATHER

DO IT AGAINST THE WALL

OR

ON THE BED?

93.

WOULD YOU RATHER

SUCK AT FOREPLAY

OR

SUCK AT SEX?

94.

WOULD YOU RATHER

WIELD THE DOMINATRIX WHIP

OR

BE WHIPPED?

95.

WOULD YOU RATHER

HAVE A DRAWER FULL OF SEX TOYS

OR

KINKY OUTFITS?

96.

WOULD YOU RATHER

HAVE SEX ON THE KITCHEN TABLE

OR

THE WASHING MACHINE?

97.

WOULD YOU RATHER

HAVE THE ABILITY TO HAVE MULTIPLE ORGASMS ON COMMAND

OR

HAVE ORGASMS THAT LAST FOR HOURS?

98.

WOULD YOU RATHER

USE NUTELLA IN SEXUAL FOOD PLAY

OR

MAPLE SYRUP?

99.

WOULD YOU RATHER

HAVE A HAPPY FIVE-YEAR RELATIONSHIP

OR

A ONE-NIGHT STAND WITH YOUR CELEBRITY CRUSH?

100.

WOULD YOU RATHER

ACCIDENTALLY FART DURING SEX

OR

DURING A BIG JOB PRESENTATION?

101.

WOULD YOU RATHER

WAKE UP NEXT TO A STRANGER

OR

HAVE AN ORGY WITH ALL YOUR FRIENDS?

102.

WOULD YOU RATHER

YOUR LEGS BE HANDCUFFED TO THE BED

OR

YOUR ARMS?

End Note

Thanks for taking the time to read our book. We hope you enjoyed reading it as much as we enjoyed researching, writing and publishing it. If you did find the book interesting please share it with your friends and family. Also look out for future publications from Relight Publishing.

Made in the USA
Monee, IL
15 April 2024